# THE MAGIC FIRE

An Adaptation of Manly Palmer Hall's Book,
## THE SECRET DESTINY OF AMERICA

by
JUDSON HARRISS

Illustrated by
DRUMMOND RIDDELL

THE PHILOSOPHICAL RESEARCH SOCIETY, INC.
Los Angeles, California

ISBN NO. 0-89314-421-5
L.C. 86-25174


Copyright © 1986
By the Philosophical Research Society, Inc.

The Philosophical Research Society acknowledges with gratitude
the gift from the author of the rights to and proceeds from
the publication of this book.

Library of Congress Cataloging-in-Publication Data

Harriss, Judson, 1915-
    The magic fire.

    Summary: An adaptation for younger readers from the
Secret destiny of America by Manly Palmer Hall.
    1. United States—History—Juvenile literature. 2. National
characteristics, American—Juvenile literature.    [1. United
States—History.    2. America—History.    3. National
characteristics, American]
    I. Hall, Manly Palmer, 1901-    . Secret destiny of America.
    II. Riddell, Drummond, ill. III. Title.

E179.H32  1986                    973                    86-25174
ISBN 0-89314-421-5

Published by
THE PHILOSOPHICAL RESEARCH SOCIETY, INC.
3910 Los Feliz Boulevard, Los Angeles, CA 90027
Printed in the U.S.A.

This little book is dedicated to
America's young people,
in whom lie the hopes and dreams
of ages past.

# ACKNOWLEDGMENTS

Following a suggestion from a friend some months ago that I undertake a version of Manly Palmer Hall's book, *The Secret Destiny of America,* for my friends of younger years, I set to work and, with considerable trepidation, produced the following story.

I am deeply grateful to Mr. Drummond Riddell who provided the marvelous drawings to illustrate this work and all thanks are due Mr. Hall for his inspiration and encouragement in our attempt to adapt his remarkable account of our beloved country's destined greatness.

Judson Harriss<br>
Los Angeles, California<br>
July 1, 1985

*"I light my candle from their torches."*
*Anatomy of Melancholy,* Robert Burton
Partition III, Section 2, Number 5, Subsection 1.

On Wednesday, December 2, 1942, a man walked out onto the stage of Carnegie Hall in New York, sat down, and began to talk.

That man was the philosopher, Manly Palmer Hall, and from this lecture came the theme for Mr. Hall's book, *The Secret Destiny of America.*

The book you hold in your hands is based upon that publication.

Any mistakes in this work are mine, not Mr. Hall's.

J.H.

# CONTENTS

Page

## LIST OF ILLUSTRATIONS

# FOREWORD

This is the story of the Unifying Power of the Eternal Flame.

And the secret of the Magic Fire is that we are One with every word you read.

J.H.

# INTRODUCTION

A Greek athlete named Koroebos was the winner of a foot race, the only event in the first Olympic Games, held about 2,760 years ago in Olympia, Greece. Legend has it that the Games were begun by Hercules, celebrating his victory over King Augeas, who had assigned Hercules the task of cleaning out the royal stables in one day. Hercules did it by sending the River Alpheus through the stables. From then on, the Greeks numbered their years in groups of four called Olympiads.

The Games grew and flourished for twelve centuries until stopped by Emperor Theodosius of Rome.

The modern Games began in Athens, Greece, in 1896, and were then held every four years in different cities, except for the VIth Olympiad scheduled in 1916 in Berlin, cancelled because of World War I.

The Xth Olympiad was held in 1932 in Los Angeles, which again, fifty-two years later, hosted another, the XXIIIrd. The XIIth and XIIIth in 1940 and 1944 were cancelled because of the Second World War.

On May 8, 1984, the sun once again kindled a flame in Olympia which was the source of fire for ten thousand American torches carried through all fifty states, ending in the lighting of the giant torch in the Los Angeles Memorial Coliseum on July 28.

Why am I telling you this?

Because the Olympic Flame is closely connected with the story of the Magic Fire.

Let us hope there will never be another cancellation of the Olympic Games due to war.

Ready? Let's start our Journey.

# ONE

# THE UNIVERSAL LIGHT
## And How It Affects Each One of Us

One evening, years ago, when I was about your age, my father and I were sitting together, talking. We had talked about many things that day: sports, school, life in our little town in the Midwest and, in particular, the sermon our preacher had given earlier that Sunday morning. I'm afraid I was a bit of a rebel in those days, and my father had been trying to nudge me gently onto a straighter path.

Dusk had fallen and the room had become dark. My father walked over to the doorway and turned on the lights. As he came back and sat down, he remarked on the miracle of light. He said, "That light in the ceiling—did you know that it gets its energy from the sun?"

I said I realized that all energy, indirectly, comes from the sun. Then he said, "And did you realize that the sun, in turn, gets its energy direct from God? The sun is the living symbol of God. It is God made visible."

Then I told him something that stopped our conversation.

I told him I didn't believe in God.

He just looked at me thoughtfully for a moment, then, without saying a word, walked over to the window, opened it, and beckoned to me. I stood silently beside him as we looked up at the night sky with its thousands of twinkling stars.

Then he flipped open the back of his old pocket watch—I can still see him do it—and let me hold it. All the little wheels and springs and levers were ticking away and working together in perfect harmony.

Finally he said, "Son, could this watch have been only an accident? Could all those little parts have just *happened* to come together?"

"Of course not," I replied, "that's ridiculous."

"How much more ridiculous," he went on, "would it be to think that those countless billions of stars, most of them bigger than our sun, could have just happened by accident? Those stars, like our own sun, have planets revolving around them like our own solar system, which is only a small part of an immense galaxy. And even this galaxy is only a tiny part of a vast cosmic clockwork, which has been moving in harmony for ages past and will continue to do so for ages to come."

He looked at me and smiled as he snapped the cover back on his gold watch.

Neither of us said another word. We didn't need to.

And I've never forgotten it.

Every time you strike a match or light a flashlight or switch on an electric light you are tapping into the energy of the sun, and—now use your imagination—you are then reaching past the blazing sun to the power *behind* the sun.

Right now I'll make you a promise. Stay with me until the end of our Journey and I'll show you a colossus with a torch, one you'll recognize right away. At the base is a beautiful poem written over a hundred years ago called—

But I'm getting ahead of myself.

That match you strike or that flashlight or light switch

you turn on light up only because of our sun, the source of energy in our solar system. And our sun, in turn, is lighted and keeps burning only because of the Universal Light, a "Cosmic Sun," . . . the Magic Fire. And that comes from God.

Let's get down to here and now before we go to our starting-point.

Did you know that this land of ours, this America, was meant to lead a free world? But we have gone through wars in the past which have badly disrupted those plans laid thousands of years ago.

The same laws that rule the movements of the stars (as well as the parts of a watch) also rule the ways we human beings conduct ourselves.

Thousands of years ago (and today too) groups of enlightened human beings gathered together to form what we might call the Order of Light-Bearers. The word "enlightened" describes someone who has seen the Universal Light and has let it shine upon his own soul.

That same Light will keep you warm-hearted too!

They knew that man has a Secret Destiny. It's secret only because we haven't seen it yet. Think of the great names in history—men like Pythagoras, Plato, Aristotle, Buddha, Jesus, Muhammad, and many others. Their teachings and writings still are powerful forces and shining examples of hope for mankind.

Did you know that this continent upon which we live today was known in Egypt thousands of years ago? And that Plato, who lived in Greece over one thousand years ago, wrote about it in his stories of Old Atlantis?

This continent was long ago destined to become the leader in the long march toward the ideal democratic state.

Democracy, a word borrowed from France and Greece,

means "government by the people."

Makes sense, doesn't it?

But the only way to get this universal brotherhood is to get rid of selfishness and learn what makes the ideal state, a nation of cooperation, not the brutal competitiveness we see today.

We can't go on trying to solve problems that always seem to keep springing up. We have to find the basic cause of our problems and solve that first.

We must realize that man is more than body, mind, and emotions. He is soul and spirit too. By the way, when I use the word "man," I mean both men and women, and boys and girls too. "Man" comes from an ancient Sanskrit word "manas," which means "mind."

Sanskrit is the ancient language of India, used in their classical and religious literature.

So, man is "the thinker" and means all of us.

Every part of man needs food. The body needs physical food, of course; the mind needs mental food, and spirit needs spiritual food. Mind needs beautiful thoughts, and spirit needs Beauty itself; beauty in our actions, in our homes, in music, art, and literature.

When you do what is right, the little spark of the Universal Flame inside each one of us burns a little brighter. You can see it shining through the windows of the soul.

And what are the windows of the soul?

The eyes of your friends!


Now coming up is the real starting-point of our adventure. We're going to shed some light on the dark pages of history as we go on.

There's an enormous pyramid looming in the distance.

You've seen it before.

It's the Great Pyramid of Gizah.

And keep this in mind as we get nearer and nearer to it.

We'll see it again at the end of our Journey.

That pyramid means we're now in Egypt, where we'll meet the world's first Light-Bearer.

*Akhnaton*

TWO
# THE LAND OF EGYPT
## And the City of the Sun

The word "pyramid" comes from a Greek word meaning "fire." Isn't that a fitting symbol for this first stop on our Journey 'round the globe? Doesn't the pyramid look like a massive flame? The Great Pyramid is an earthly symbol of the Universal Fire.

We are looking in on this ancient land during the rulership of the first man in history who saw the Universal Light and did his best to give that same Light to his people. Pictures of him often show the sun overhead shedding its rays in all directions, with each ray ending in the shape of a hand. Isn't that interesting? It shows that Akhnaton—that was the name he took—knew that the sun shone on everyone, ready to "lend a hand" to each of us.

The young king, or Pharaoh, as Egyptian kings were called, was born over one thousand years before Christ. His name originally was Amen-Hotep IV. The young prince married an Egyptian girl named Nefertiti.

When he reached the age of twenty, he saw that the old religion called Amon-Ra had become corrupt, so he began to reform it.

That angered the priests, and they plotted to kill the young king, but he escaped and built a new city 160 miles up the Nile River from Cairo, called Khut-en-Aton, which means "City of the Sun."

He then changed his name to Akhnaton and settled down with the beautiful Nefertiti, to whom he referred as "my beloved wife."

He wrote simple, beautiful poems which still exist after more than 3,000 years.

The royal couple had seven daughters, one of whom later married a young prince whose name you'll recognize. His name was Tutankhamen . . . better known as "King Tut."

I wish I could say that the family lived happily ever after, with Akhnaton ruling over a nation in peace, teaching his people that God dwells in all living things, in birds and beasts, insects and plants, as well as human beings everywhere.

But it didn't work out that way. He was too far ahead of his time. He saw God in his enemies as well as in his own people. The priests began to plot against him, and finally his country was invaded by armies from other countries.

But he refused to send soldiers to fight them.

Why? Because he saw those enemy soldiers as children of God too.

So this story has a sad ending. The armies destroyed much of Egypt and captured the cities.

And Akhnaton died at the altar of God.

He was only 36 years old.

But perhaps, my Friend, the ending isn't so sad after all.

This gentle king willingly gave his life for a dream, a dream that grew stronger with the years that followed.

That dream is alive today.

That dream, the dream of the Magic Fire, helps us all to become better men and women.

Akhnaton was truly the first Keeper of the Flame.

Before we leave this ancient land of Egypt, take a long last look back at the Great Pyramid.

Why? Because we'll be seeing it again at the end of our Journey in a most interesting way.

Now let's shine our lights to the northeast and cross the great Mediterranean Sea to another ancient land—The Land of Greece.

# THREE

# WHERE OCEAN VOYAGES BEGAN
## And Where Some of Them Ended

The Greeks of long ago hid their beliefs and discoveries in fables and stories. They knew far more about the lands and oceans than most people today realize.

One of the stories was about Atlas and his three daughters. Atlas, as you may remember, is pictured carrying the world on his shoulders.

He put his three daughters, called the Hesperides ("hess-pear-a-deez") in charge of a garden where grew a tree which bore golden apples. At the foot of the tree was coiled a dragon named Ladon.

The dragon was eventually slain by Hercules, who seized the golden apples. That was one of his "twelve labors."

The three sisters, also called the daughters of Night, lived in a blessed land where the sun came to rest at the end of each day.

And where does the sun "come to rest"?

In the west, of course.

And what is the "blessed land"?

It's the continent of North America!

A Greek named Plutarch wrote about voyages over the ocean to these western lands. A look at the world map shows that a ship sailing west from Greece across the Mediterranean Sea through the Strait of Gibraltar and on across the Atlantic Ocean will reach the eastern shores of North America. Plutarch described what must have been the St. Laurence River and our Great Lakes region.

And that was long before the days of Columbus!

Another Greek writer, a famous philosopher named Plato, also wrote about the "Western Paradise." We'll learn more about him later on in our Journey.

Star clusters called constellations were given names by the ancient astronomers. The star group which hovers over North America was named "the eagle." The star group over Mexico and Central America was named "the serpent." We'll learn more about that story too in the legends the ancient writers left for us.

You've noticed, I'm sure, that the Chinese and Japanese people often use the dragon in their stories and paintings.

And what cluster of stars coils over those two countries?

"The dragon," of course!

Here's one more example; the constellation over Russia is called "the great bear." The bear has long been the symbol of Russia, and was the mascot of the 1980 Olympic Games in Moscow.

And, as you know, the official mascot of the Games held in 1984 in Los Angeles was the eagle.

There is an old legend about "The Golden Fleece" and the search for it led by a sailor named Jason. Most of the early explorers were simply looking for gold, a metal dug up from the earth.

But the word "fleece" means the wool from a sheep,

and "The Golden Fleece" was the dried skin of a sheep, called parchment, upon which was written the secret of eternal life—the Universal Light.

That was what Jason *really* searched for.

And mark this well; America has its own Golden Fleece! It's the Declaration of Independence, written on the skin of an animal. The original is kept in the Library of Congress in Washington, D.C.

I suggest that you get a copy of it.

In it is the secret of eternal life of our country.

There is another "Golden Fleece"—England's Magna Charta, signed by King John in 1215, long before our own bill of human rights.

Present-day democracy is based upon those two "Golden Fleeces."

For many years after the early explorers came to these shores, the land belonged to the Indians. It was not until the 17th and 18th centuries that the people of Europe saw it as the land of freedom and opportunity. Then they began to arrive in streams, gradually shaping a new country which was destined to become the shining example of world democracy.

The fulfillment of those early settlers' dreams—the real "Golden Age"—still lies ahead.

And you're a part of it.

What a golden opportunity!

And what a challenge!

Now, with one last look back, we leave the Blessed Land of the West (for now; we'll come back again), and turn our faces to the east again.

We're going back across the ocean to Greece and another marvelous story in our Quest.

FOUR
# THE UNDERGROUND RIVER
## And the Mysterious Island

The Archon of the Athenian State 600 years before the birth of Christ was a man named Solon. He was the judge of civil and religious matters for the Athenians, and his first task was to change the old laws about private debts between the citizens.

Property lines in those days were marked by stones in the ground, and when a person on one side owed money to the person on the other side, the amount was carved into one of the stones. A very odd bookkeeping system, wasn't it? And especially rough on farmers. After a few years there were so many rocks it became hard to plow the ground.

And when some poor farmer wasn't able to pay back the money, what happened? Why, the rich landowner next door simply moved the stones farther back into the farmer's land!

If the farmer still was unable to pay, he finally became only a renter and was forced to give the rich landowner a large share of his crops.

And if he was unable to do even that? . . .

Then he became a slave, and the landowner owned everything, even the body of the farmer!

The new Archon, Solon, saw the injustice of that system, and took the first step to remedy it by freeing the

15

slaves. So right away he had one group angry at him . . . the landowners.

Then he cut the taxes the poor people had to pay.

He gave them the right to vote.

He set up the jury system and declared all citizens equal.

These and other laws were the beginning of Greek democracy.

Finally, Solon had made so many enemies (reformers have always had a hard time, haven't they?) that he was forced to give up. He resigned.

Then all the people loved and respected him again.


Being a wise man, Solon knew how little he really knew, and he wanted to know more.

He knew where to go to search for more knowledge.

He went to Egypt and talked with the temple priests.

The High Priest told him, "You Greeks are children; you have not yet learned what the gods have taught."

The High Priest led him down a flight of stairs to a tunnel beneath the temple lighted by torches, on down stone steps worn smooth by time, to a river flowing through underground caves.

The river was the Nile. A black boat was moored to the landing. Men were sitting in it, waiting. When Solon and the priest stepped into the boat, the men began to row silently over the black waters.

Then Solon noticed that the men were blind.

The boat came to a stop at the foot of a tiny island on which were twin columns with a polished surface that glistened in the light of the flickering torches. The two men stepped out of the boat and approached the two pillars, on which was writing in a strange language. The priest pointed his rod of gold at the writing and said, "These two columns were built thousands of years ago by people who have vanished from the earth.

"They are made of a metal which will shine brightly forever. We have learned how to read the words. They tell of rules which must be obeyed by all nations. When any nation breaks the rules etched upon these pillars, that nation dies.

"You see, my son," the High Priest continued, "once upon a time there was a great nation on land rising from the Atlantic Ocean. It was ruled by seven kings who lived in peace, working together in harmony.

"Giant ships sailed in and out of their chief city, known as The Golden Gate.

"But there came a time when these kings became ambitious. They wanted to rule the whole world. They left their peaceful kingdoms to make war on the lands to the east, to Europe, where terrible battles were fought.

"That angered the gods, who then caused a devastating earthquake, and in one single night the seven kingdoms sank into the ocean and disappeared. Just think! Sixty million human beings were drowned because they had broken the laws etched upon these two columns."

Much affected, Solon sadly returned to the boat after the High Priest ended his story.

How terrible that earthquake must have been!

And how bad must have been the conduct of the people of those seven kingdoms to result in such a tragedy.

Doesn't it serve as a warning to us today to try to find those rules and live by them?

You and I don't need to stand before those two metal

pillars in Egypt. The rules have been preserved for us, and the purpose of this Journey you are on is to find them.

Solon sailed back to Greece, intending to write down all that he had learned, but by that time he was becoming old and feeble, so he told the story to his closest friend, a man named Dropis.

Dropis told it to his son, Critias, who passed it on to his grandson, who was also named Critias.

This grandson later became a disciple to a famous teacher, Socrates.

The talk between these two has a name . . . "Critias."

On our next stop we'll shed more light on the story of the seven kingdoms and how they came to be destroyed so suddenly.

The land of those kingdoms was Old Atlantis.

*Atlantis*

# FIVE

# THE DESTRUCTION OF OLD ATLANTIS
## The Story of Ten Kings

Plato, the Greek Philosopher, wrote down the story of the lost kingdom of Atlantis, as we learned in our visit to that Egyptian temple. It took the form of a talk between Socrates and his disciple, Critias.

Following are the main parts of the story. In it we find out what happens when laws are broken.

Once upon a time there lived ten kings who ruled over seven islands and three continents. All those lands together made up what we now call Atlantis.

The ten kings had long ruled in peace, obedient to the laws of Poseidon, god of the seas.

This long-ago time was a Golden Age, a time when the peoples of the earth were unselfish and cooperative, obeying the laws of Heaven as best they could.

The three great continents were Europe, Asia, and Africa.

The "seven islands" were the rest of the earth.

Plato taught that the best and wisest should govern the rest, and that anyone, through hard work and study and right actions could become wise. So wisdom is up to you, and no one can keep you from it.

In that way, rightful rulers of man are made, and peace

is the result.

But when leaders become greedy and compete with each other, war follows closely behind.

For a long time the people of Atlantis did live in peace. There were great schools in beautiful cities, with parks and open spaces set aside for the enjoyment of the citizens among the beauties of Nature.

There was little crime, so there was little to fear. The people worked in cooperation and enjoyed their leisure times.

Poseidon rewarded them with good climates, rich soils, and all the bounties that Nature provides.

How sad to learn that the time of peace ended.

Gradually, the people became selfish. They began to want more and became resentful of others' prosperity.

This jealousy and this grasping of more and more broke out in petty squabbles and bickering which increased day by day, spreading like wildfire.

Finally the kings themselves grew so jealous of each other that they no longer gathered together in peaceful co-operation and goodwill. Secretly, each of them had the desire to rule all of the others.

When kings become tyrants, there is only one possible result. . . .

War!

As we have seen, the seven kings of Atlantis formed armies and set sail eastward toward Europe, bent on conquest. They eventually fought their way as far as Greece itself.

At that point, Zeus, the father of all the gods, seeing all

the natural laws being broken, called the other eleven gods to a meeting on Mount Olympus.

When they had all assembled, Zeus stood up and said. . . .

Right there is where Plato ended his story, leaving it to our imagination as to what Zeus said.

So we don't know what he *said,* but we certainly do know what he *did.*

He hurled his thunderbolt down upon Atlantis and destroyed it with earthquakes and terrible fires.

Ever since that day, men have believed that peace is impossible and that war and crime are natural and inevitable.

But Plato knew that the Golden Age could come again and would come again, far in the future.

To that end he established a school at Athens, where he taught religion, philosophy, and science.

The Old Atlantis had disappeared forever, but the records of Atlantis are preserved on two shining columns under that temple in Egypt.

Now, my Friend, did you know there is a New Atlantis? Yes, more than 2,000 years after Solon gazed upon that strange language by the flickering light of his torch, another philosopher in England described the perfect government of a beautiful country in a book called *New Atlantis.*

I'm finding my heart beating more rapidly as I look forward to exploring the founding of that country with you later on.

For now, let's shine our lights toward the west again, toward The Eternal City . . . Rome.

## SIX

# A GAME OF CHESS
## And What Almost Happened

Seven hundred years after the time of Plato, a 40-year-old Egyptian philosopher named Plotinus went to live in Rome. He was a friend and advisor of the Roman Emperor Galienus, and had been studying the writings of Plato.

The two men liked to play chess together, and they discussed affairs of state while they played. During one game, Plotinus suggested that the deserted ruins of an ancient city near Rome be rebuilt and used for the advancement of learning.

The passage of many years and destruction at the hands of vandals had left the old city in shambles, with only a shadow remaining of its former splendor.

Plotinus described the projected city, which he suggested be named "Platonopolis," and what it would mean to the Roman Empire. It would be a city of the wise, a magnet for men of learning the world over, and would bring honor to Rome and to the Emperor himself.

That sounded reasonable to Galienus, and the more he listened and thought about it, the better he liked the idea. He decided to go ahead and build the city.

He went to the Roman Senate with the plans. And there the project came to a grinding halt. The Senators turned it down after whispered meetings, and Galienus found out that he lacked the power he may have thought he had. The

Senators told him that if he insisted on the project, they would choose some other more reasonable ruler.

Now why did the plan fail?

It failed because the Senators were afraid of losing their own power. Their reasoning went something like this in their discussions: "Look, if this new city were full of wise men, what would become of us? Why, we'd become second-rate. And the Empire would collapse!"

So they voted against the plan and sailed blindly along in the same old way, little knowing that the Roman Empire was about to fall in a very few years anyway.

By the way, did you know that history shows that empires—what we call "great powers" today—stay in power only about 250 years? They go through a period of growth, then wealth and power, followed by decay and finally collapse. Why does this happen? Well, as we have just seen, and will see on our Journey ahead, the collapse comes from within first, like a fruit rotting on the inside.

This country of ours, remember, is now over 200 years old. Can the decay and collapse be prevented here? Surely so.

The big question is . . . *will* it be prevented here?

The answer to that, my young Friend, is up to you and your generation. The Great Plan to guide you will be seen more clearly as we go along.

Let's go back to the chess games the two men went on playing. Both of them dreamed of the City of the Wise, but found they could only talk about it.

They played chess and talked.

Rome was about to be destroyed.

It's the same old story; wise men could lead us onto new paths of glory, but ignorant men block the way.

But take heart; good men never die. Plato's words are heard and discussed more widely today than when he lived.

Wars and crime, through the centuries, have often reduced centers of civilization to rubble.

This is madness, and surely will, some day, come to an end.

You and your generation could make Plato's and Plotinus' dreams come true—dreams of great institutions of learning drawing dedicated people together. There the twin columns of Truth and Justice would support the Brotherhood of Man, where the wise would gather and swear to obey Universal Law.

This Law and this oath would bring people together.

War would soon be only a bad dream in memory.

Today, every great nation has fine schools.

These schools and these nations can and should cooperate.

They need a shining ideal, a guiding light.

That's just what our Journey, O my Companion, is about.

So let's get on with it.

SEVEN
# THE FIRE THAT WILL NOT DIE
## The Story of the Guilds

In 1984 the Eternal Flame . . . the sun . . . kindled the Olympic Flame in Olympia, Greece.

That flame was relayed to Athens by more than 675 young athletes, then was flown to New York, where the run to Los Angeles began on May 8.

Ten thousand Americans carried that flame through all 50 states before finally lighting the giant torch in Los Angeles' Memorial Coliseum on July 28.

In the same way, for thousands of years, men and women who seek Truth have gone directly to the Eternal Light . . . God . . . and have lit their own little torches (their minds and hearts) and passed the light on to others.

These others, in turn, pass the flame on to still others, and so on, down through the ages.

Those early Torch-Bearers, in order to keep the Light of Truth alive, found it necessary to band together in secret groups. They had to be secret because of persecution by the ignorant. And they will keep on working in secrecy until it is no longer necessary.

These groups, the Order of the Quest, are scattered all over the globe, in China, India, Arabia, Africa, and the Eskimos in the north.

These various bands are formed under widely differing conditions, and with different goals.

One group started in Greece more than 3,000 years ago. They were the men who built the temples and stadiums, theaters and government buildings. They were stone-cutters.

If you've seen pictures of diamonds as they are dug up from the ground, you'll agree that they look like little ordinary, rough pebbles.

But take a look at these same diamonds after they've been cut, smoothed, and polished. Beautiful, aren't they, as they refract the sunlight in brilliant colors.

Well, the real purpose of the stone-cutters who banded together was to take rough, crude, ignorant *human beings* and smooth and polish *them* until they shone like finished diamonds, reflecting Truth, the Light of God.

The stone-cutters take the chunks of rocks dug up from the ground and cut and smooth them so they fit together perfectly to build a temple.

A temple built of uncut rocks wouldn't last very long, would it, before collapsing.

In the same way, a nation made up of rough (ignorant) people would soon fall apart too, but if these same people (diamonds in the rough) were made smooth and true they could fit together to build a great nation.

There is a legend that King Solomon's temple was built without hammer and nails. That temple is really the perfect nation, each "stone" being a refined and perfected human being.

The skilled stone-cutters put their secret mark on each stone.

And God puts his mark on each human being, a mark for all with eyes to see.

Beautiful story, isn't it?

When the light from the Magic Fire reached the Romans, they named their guild the Collegia. The head of the Collegians was a man named Vitruvious. He was the designer of the famous Roman aqueducts, the water transportation system still seen today.

The rise of the Christian Church, with its persecution of the old pagan beliefs, caused the secret societies to become even more secret. The different groups were swallowed up by the Church, but they kept their ideas and merely changed names to conform, on the surface, to the new theology. Underneath, the Fire burned as brightly as ever, and the flames of Truth were passed along from member to member, just as the Olympic runners do.

The Torch-Bearers travelled eastward from Rome to Arabia and India. Through the years they left their marks on stones in temples, palaces, and mosques.

In Europe the Torch-Bearers formed groups of architects, masons, wood-carvers, and glass-makers, all of whom worked together to build the magnificent cathedrals that we gaze at in wonder and awe today.

The perfect nation would be like one of those great cathedrals with all of its parts (the citizens) fitting together to make a perfect union, with all the professions, trades, and crafts working together in harmony.

Throughout the ages, chemists have searched for a medicine to cure man's ailments. This search for that medicine is called alchemy, which really means "divine chemistry," and the searchers are called alchemists.

*Alchemist*

What is the medicine? Truth, which would (and does) cure man's illnesses.

The wise man's "stone" is Science.

The alchemists did try to find a substance which would turn lead into gold. But that's the least important part of the search, only a symbol of the deeper search.

You see, the "lead" is actually an ignorant person.

And "gold" is the perfected human being.

Our Light-Bearers are everywhere.

One group looked for the "pearl of great price" . . . wisdom.

Another sought for The Holy Grail, which was the cup used by Jesus at the Last Supper with his disciples. That, too, is highly symbolic. Perhaps the real "Holy Grail" is the human heart.

Another group of men and women formed the Society of the Rose Cross.

If you take the word "rose" and place the "e" in front, it becomes "eros," a Greek word meaning "love."

Actually, all of these groups belong to one large society, the Order of the Quest.

Quest means "search" or "journey" like the one you and I are on. And isn't life itself a "quest"?

What is behind all this searching? Happiness.

But happiness can never be found by searching for it alone. It has to be earned. Our Declaration of Independence says that one of the rights given to us by God is the *pursuit* of happiness.

Happiness is a "by-product" of obedience to the Laws of God.

When you do something worthwhile, when you are able to really help someone in trouble, you feel happy, don't you? That's what it's all about.

One of our honored Light-Bearers was an Englishman named Elias Ashmole, who lived in the 17th century. Through his writings we understand more of the true purpose of the Master Masons. A mason is someone who works with stones, but Sir Elias helped lift the symbolism of the guilds beyond the physical, to the mental and soul levels.

The secret societies exist today, and will do so until the Quest is complete.

In the meantime, you and I must keep our own Torches burning and pass on our little flames to those still groping in the dark.

# EIGHT

# THE SEARCH FOR CHRISTOPHER COLUMBUS
## An Unsolved Puzzle

You'll notice our title is . . . the *Search* for Christopher Columbus. The reason is that we know very little about one of the most famous men in history.

How can that be?

Well, evidence thus far uncovered points to the fact that Columbus was not an uneducated Italian of humble station, as is often believed, but was, rather, a Greek with excellent classical education.*

And, to add an interesting sidelight, he was accompanied on his voyage by a stranger who went along as an advisor. The stranger did not return, but stayed in the West Indies. It's quite possible that the stranger was one of our Torch-Bearers, a member of the Order of the Quest.

What are the known facts about our famous explorer, Columbus?

His birth is unrecorded.

And where was he born? We don't know. Twenty cities claim Columbus as a native son!

In 1937 a little book by one Spyros Cateras was published, called *Christopher Columbus Was a Greek*. The

---

*See *The Secret Destiny of America,* by Manly P. Hall.

author says Columbus' real name was NIKOLAOS YPSI-LANTIS, and he quotes from historical documents.

Of one thing we feel sure:

Greek explorers had reached South America long before Christ was born. And according to the book mentioned above, there are traces of Alexander the Great's army in Uruguay.

An educated Greek of that day would have been well acquainted with the writings of Plato. Scholars were well aware that the earth was a ball, not a flat plate.

Columbus' own son referred to his father as a Greek!

Those were days of great changes and new ideas.

Europe was emerging from the Dark Ages into the dawn of a new day. The Magic Fire was reaching into the globe's dark corners.

Printing had been invented—a big step forward.

Democracy was still an infant, but growing.

Tribes were forming into nations.

What was needed right then?

Why, a new world concept.

And always, when something is badly needed, it is available, and a Light-Bearer will find it.

Today we are again searching for a new world.

What kind? There are no new continents to be discovered, are there?

Ah, but there is one—the unknown continent of the mind.

*Socrates*

If we can send a man to the moon, and beyond, we can also explore this mental continent.

The word "psyche" means "mind." And psychology, the study of the mind, is really just beginning.

After Columbus' day, more was known about our earth. More people came to understand that it was a globe.

And more important, more and more people today understand that the earth is a unit . . . one world.

Far greater voyages than Columbus took lie ahead of us. For one thing, there will be more explorations of outer space.

But, most important of all, there will be *inner* space explorations, into our hearts, minds, souls, spirit.

Socrates said that we live on the shore of a land we know nothing about, a land filled with treasures, treasures enjoyed by the wise.

Let's see if we can join them ourselves—shall we?

At least, for now, we can learn more about them.

And isn't that a joyful journey itself?

So let's go.

NINE
# THE MAN WHO SAW
# 400 YEARS AHEAD
## Using "A Slender Flame"

In 1503, eleven years after Columbus' famous voyage, a man named Michel Nostradamus was born in France. He became a doctor, but is better known as a prophet. His range of visions extended more than 400 years ahead, clear to the end of our present century. Some of his predictions are yet to be fulfilled.

He hid his predictions in little verses called quatrains, which have puzzled his readers for centuries, because he purposely wrote them down in such an obscure way that they are understood only after the events take place.

For instance, he once called America (he used that exact word) "The Land Which Keeps the Thursday."

That would be our Thanksgiving, of course.

What he really wanted to do was to spread the Light, not to alarm people. He wanted them to be wiser and better.

He must have been one of our Torch-Bearers, a member of the Order of the Quest.

Here is his very first quatrain:

Seated at night in my secret study,
Alone reposing over the brass tripod

39

A slender flame leaps out of the solitude,
Making me pronounce that which is not in vain.
                    Century I, Quatrain 1.

He referred to America as "The Blessed Isles of the West."

He predicted that America would break away from the mother country (England) and live in peace with its sister (Canada).

He saw our country fighting several wars, one of them being against the Orient. The word "orient" comes from Latin and French words meaning "east" or "land of rising sun."

That war, he said, would pit "the eagle" (the United States) against "the rising sun" (Japan).

How did he do it? We may never know, but for years to come, scholars will still be puzzling over his strange verses, matching his predictions with events as they occur.


Another prophet, also a doctor, but not as well-known as Nostradamus, lived in England 200 years ago. His name was Ebenezar Sibly. We're told that he shut himself up in a little room to get away from his nagging wife. In the solitude of his room he studied and wrote books on medicine and astrology.

Perhaps Mrs. Sibly was glad Dr. Sibly stayed in his room and out of her way. Anyhow, we know she must have been a patient, forgiving woman, because she passed his meals to him through a hole in the door.


Those were the days when our country was just being born, and most British leaders were sure the rebellious little colonies would soon be begging for mercy and to be allowed to come back into the commonwealth.

"No," said Dr. Sibly, "the American colonies will not come back. They have broken away for good, and will some day be rich and powerful, even . . ." and this must have surprised the British politicians, ". . . more powerful than England!"

The ancients studied astrology to learn how to build better governments. They knew that the motions of the heavenly bodies set great patterns of natural laws.

Let me tell you a little story:

One day I was talking with a friend of mine, a scientist, about the solar system. I remarked how wonderful it was that God kept it whirling so beautifully through Space.

"Nonsense!" he exclaimed. "I'll show you just what your solar system is." He filled a large bowl with water and placed a spoonful of oil on the surface.

Then he put his finger in the water and moved it around and around. The spoonful of oil broke up into a large central drop with other smaller drops circling around it.

"There's your solar system," he said triumphantly, looking over at me. "That's all there is to it!"

I smiled back at him and answered, "Tell me, my friend, what's going to happen when you take your finger out of that bowl?"

He didn't reply for a moment, as he watched the little drops of oil circling around.

Then he stopped, and we both silently watched as the little drops all came together again with the central drop, and the spoonful of oil rotated slowly, then came to a stop in the center of the bowl.

You've seen cartoons where the artist drew a light bulb

over some person who has just gotten a "bright idea," haven't you? That's what I pictured as my friend said, after a few minutes, "I see what you mean. Perhaps you're right. Perhaps it is the 'finger of God' that keeps the whole system going." He never again laughed at the idea of God keeping the planets moving in their orbits around the sun.

I believe those old astrologers were really members of the Order of the Quest. They were often used as advisors to kings and queens, like Merlin in King Arthur's court. They had great influence and helped bring about necessary changes in government. Their studies and writings make our own lives much better today.

Let's not forget the strange little verses of Nostradamus. They will still be important to us for years to come. One of his important predictions was the formation of the United Nations, the hope of peace, a time when men and nations could live together in harmony.

Surely the world will soon be a planet of peace.

It certainly could be. Nostradamus and the many other Light-Bearers dreamed and pointed the way.

We can make those dreams come true.

But will we?

THE LAND OF NOWHERE
The Book of Dreams

There is a well-known book (but very few have read it!) called *Utopia*. It was written in 1516 by an Englishman named Thomas More. "Utopia" is an imaginary island where people live in a perfect society. The word has come to mean any ideal place or condition.

Sir Thomas More got his idea for the book from our old friend Plato and his book called *Republic*. *Utopia* was very popular soon after being written, as it was also an attack on the famous English monarch, King Henry VIII, who, as you may remember, had six wives, two of whom were beheaded. More himself was eventually beheaded by King Henry.

Another "Utopian" was an Italian named Campanella, who lived a century later. He wrote a book called *Civitas Solis,* which means "City of the Sun."

He was a scientist, and he also described what he saw as an ideal city, a place where the citizens shared equally in the prosperity of the state and elected leaders on their merit. His ideas also followed the writings of Plato. The rulers of a perfect state would really have little to do, as the citizens would govern themselves in complete freedom.

Also in Italy lived another writer, a man named Boccalini, who wrote a story about Apollo, god of light, who tried to reform the human race.

Finally Apollo gave up and said it couldn't be done. He was tired from his efforts, and decided on a much easier task. He thought maybe he could at least keep down the price of cabbages!

That reminds me of George Washington Carver, a black man whose parents had been slaves. He looked up at heaven one day and said, "Lord, I want to know everything."

The Lord looked down at him and replied, "George, you're asking too much."

Carver thought for a moment, then said, "Lord, I want to know everything . . . about the peanut!"

And the Lord replied, "Now you're talking, George."

So Carver began his famous experiments with the peanut. From it he made a surprisingly large number of products, including cheese, milk, coffee, flour, ink, dyes, soap, and many other things, all from the peanut. Isn't that amazing?

We don't need to know everything all at once. It's like the man who became impatient with the slow growth of a rosebud, and opened it up himself so he could enjoy the full-blown beauty immediately. So what happened? It died, of course. What we do need to do is use wisely what we do know, and to keep on learning more, day by day.

Back to Boccalini. This Rosicrucian story tells us we must first see our faults, then correct them, then form a better government, and then educate the politicians. Sounds like a rather big job, doesn't it?

Boccalini wasn't popular. No reformer is. He may even have been killed by his enemies.

Germany had a famous Rosicrucian Utopian named Johann Valentin Andrea, who wrote a book called *Christianopolis,* which means "City of Christ." He got his ideas from Plotinus. Remember Plotinus' city called "Platonopolis"? Andrea's book is the story of a city without poverty, a city where the arts and sciences flourish and all the citizens lead contented, peaceful lives.

Andrea is showing us that men and women everywhere, right in our own cities today, could work together in harmony and bring about a future bright with happiness.

Before we leave this "land of nowhere" . . . by the way, the word "utopia" is an interesting one. It comes from a Latin word meaning "no place." Unfortunately, the word utopia has come to mean places or schemes that are totally unworkable; idle dreams not humanly possible to attain.

But the word "nowhere" can be broken down into the two words "now" and "here." In other words, the dreams of the old Utopians actually could be realized here and now, if we'd just do it.

But as I started to say, before we leave the land of "nowhere," I'll give you a hint at what lies just ahead of us.

We're going to look in upon a man whose magic fire still brightens our lives today, a fire which sheds light on history as it's being written.

He wrote a book called *New Atlantis,* but it wasn't finished . . . or was it? Maybe the last part was held back because society wasn't ready for it.

Perhaps, in the near future, it will come to light. I hope you will be able to read it yourself some day.

Anyway, the part that was published gives us plenty to think about and work on, as we shall see.

We've reached the half-way point in our Journey, and we've seen a lot, but, O my Companion, just wait and see what lies ahead. The best part is yet to come. You and I will ssee the dreams of the ancients coming true in a fascinating way.

We'll see that Utopia is really here . . . now!

But we must move on.

Stay with me.

*Francis Bacon*

# ELEVEN

# PAST THE TWIN PILLARS
# OF HERCULES
## At Home in Solomon's House

Sir Francis Bacon, who lit the lamp of learning in the days of Shakespeare, lived in England from 1561 to 1626. Those 65 years produced an enormous amount of writing. One of his books, already mentioned, was *New Atlantis,* printed one year after Bacon's death by his friend William Rawley.

At the front of the book is a curious picture. It shows an old man persuading a woman to come out of her cave.

The old man is Father Time.

The woman is Truth.

And we do learn the Truth through Time, don't we? As we work through the years, we do, at last, see Truth in the light of day, as it is drawn out of the dark night of the Cave of Ignorance.

A simple picture like that is a good way to tell a story. It helps us see what we so often try in vain to hear in the use of mere words.

And that drawing is one of the symbols of the Order of the Quest. A symbol is a mark, or sign, a picture that tells a story. For example, the lion is often used as a symbol of bravery.

And you and I use the Torch-Bearer as a symbol of the

men and women who dream of, and work toward, the perfection of mankind.

Mr. Rawley wrote a short note of explanation at the front of *New Atlantis*. He said the book was about the "college of the six days' work." This "college," which is really the whole world, is called "Solomon's House."

The world, as we read in the Bible, was created by God in six days.

So this place we live in and this time we live in are a "semester" in that school. We're supposed to work and grow and graduate to the next grade.

As we have seen, *New Atlantis* is unfinished. But the Torch-Bearers believe that the second part really was written. They say it tells about a great room in Solomon's House where real members of the Order of the Quest are named. Perhaps it's buried in a vault, just waiting for Father Time to open it up and draw it out into the pure light of day.

Perhaps the real reason the second part wasn't published is that those members named would have been persecuted at that time.

Once upon a time, a ship set sail over the ocean from Peru in South America, bound for China and Japan. A great storm arose and drove the ship far off its course, causing danger of death by starvation. The sailors prayed to God for help, and their prayers were answered. The ship arrived safely in a fair harbor of a great city in an unknown land.

That reads very much like the opening scene in Shakespeare's play, *The Tempest*, where a great storm came up and drove a ship far off its course.

By the magic power of a man named Prospero, the ship was brought safely into the harbor of an unknown island.

That play was written about the same time as *New Atlantis*.

Surely the stories were connected!

Another drawing in one of Bacon's books shows a ship sailing out to sea between two columns, which are really the "Pillars of Hercules" in the Strait of Gibraltar. They are the two tips of land—the southern tip of Spain and the northern tip of Morocco—that come close together at the western end of the Mediterranean Sea.

To sail out into the Atlantic Ocean from the Mediterranean, a ship has to pass those two pillars.

What is the ship? Science.

What is the Mediterranean? The old world.

What is the Atlantic Ocean? The new world.

Our Journey together is filled with stories of ships, isn't it? A ship is a symbol of knowledge, in which we can sail from the dark land of ignorance to the fair harbor of wisdom. And the voyage doesn't have to be dangerous, with storms that blow us off our course. It can be filled with blue skies and gentle winds. Life is what we make of it.

Bacon's little ship arrived safely in the harbor of the City of the Wise in the land called Bensalem, which means "Son of Peace."

Bensalem sent goods to other lands.

What goods? Why, the Light of Truth!

One of those lands was Atlantis.

And what is Atlantis? America!

The college of Solomon's House sent Light-Bearers all over the world, storing their knowledge in great libraries.

*New Atlantis* ends with a talk by one of the teachers in the House of Solomon. He tells about great schools and libraries, parks, concert halls, hospitals, observatories, gardens and museums.

All these were to be set up in the "Wise Men's Cities" to search for causes, to educate, to make man wise and help him to grow. The final aim was perfection.

The story ends suddenly.

The last part of *New Atlantis,* if indeed it was written down, has not yet been found.

Bacon's dream was that his college would be set up in America.

Much of his dream has come true. We do have great universities, laboratories, libraries, and museums.

We do have gardens and parks and concert halls.

We have split the atom and sent men to the moon.

What more do we need? Philosophy.

We need to know the rules we must follow to make the dream come true . . . the rules in the missing part of Bacon's *New Atlantis.*

The rules *are* known . . . to a few.

They will soon, I hope, be known to many more.

And you, my Companion, can be one of them.

The time has come for us to leave Sir Francis, but only

for a little while. We'll see things in our next adventure which will set the stage for his return.

For now, with one last look back at the twin Pillars of Hercules, we're sailing westward over the great Atlantic Ocean toward the New World.

*Quetzalcoatl*

# TWELVE

# THE STORY OF THE FEATHERED SERPENT
## Back Home to Stay

Over 100 cities were swallowed up by the jungles of Central America. These ancient ruins, still being explored, were the pride of a now lost civilization that flourished 1,000 years before Columbus landed on these eastern shores. Little is known about the land of the Mayas—that's what they were called—because the records and historical writings were destroyed by the Spanish explorers.

One thing the Mayas left behind for us was the legend of an old man who came from the sea, riding on a raft of snakes.

The Mayan people who lived in what is now Mexico named him Quetzalcoatl, which means "feathered serpent."

Quetzal was the name of a bird of the Mayas, and "coatl" means "snake," so Quetzalcoatl is "the snake covered with feathers of the quetzal bird." He came from the east, from the "land of many colored rocks."

The Feathered Serpent stayed in the land for years, teaching the people laws of government, languages, arts, religion, medicine and agriculture.

Then one day he walked to the seashore, called to his raft of snakes, and sailed away over the ocean to the east. Before he left, though, he promised the people he would return some day.

That promise led to a great tragedy.

You see, the story was kept alive through the years, and when Cortez, leader of the Spanish explorers, landed many years later, King Montezuma thought it was Quetzalcoatl returning, and he handed over his crown of feathers to the Spanish leader.

Quite a story, isn't it?

But the story has a sad ending. Much of this old civilization was destroyed in the early years of the Spanish conquest. Murder, removal of treasures, and the destruction of old records took place, then the ravages of time did the rest.

Let's look at the bright side of the picture.

The Mayas set up the first democracy on this continent. The rulers seem to have been wise and the priests good. The people worshipped The One God, whose home was the sun.

Now doesn't that remind you of Akhnaton?

In our Journey through Time we have seen people worshipping different gods. Every time, though, even when many gods are worshipped, there is still just The One God who rules over all.

Come to think of it, if a belief in those minor deities makes us better men and women . . . why not? Wouldn't it be better, for instance, to visualize little deities of our garden or our kitchen, and so try to keep our garden and our kitchen clean and orderly, than to *refuse* to imagine them and *neglect* our gardens and homes? Doesn't that make sense?

Next to The One God, the Mayas worshipped the Feathered Serpent, whom they believed to be a kind of savior who suffered, died, and rose again.

The Mayas hold the world record for peace . . . 500 years. They shared equally in all things, and were safe as long as they obeyed the laws given them by the Feathered Serpent.

And here's an unusual fact—they didn't use money! Maybe that's why they were able to live in peace for so long.

And here's something else curious; to them, the wheel was the symbol of death, so they had no machines.

There was no poverty, and there must have been little or no crime, because no signs of prisons have ever been found.

They believed that each man's religion was his own business. When they saw that a man was good, they knew that his religion had to be good . . . whatever it was.

Other tribes in South America and our own North American Indian tribes held similar beliefs. The Indians never advanced as far as the Mayas, but they did take care of their old people, the sick, and the orphans. Crime was almost unknown. Because the tribes moved about so much and came into conflict with other tribes, battles did often occur, but these seem to have taken place on a high level of rules of combat.

Later on, seven of the Indian tribes formed the first League of Nations in the Great Lakes region under a chief named "Great Rabbit," mentioned in Longfellow's "Hiawatha."

They were beginning to live in peace.

The Incas, from Peru in South America, also formed an

empire. Some of their villages still exist today.

All of this shows us that the thirteen American colonies declaring themselves a free and independent nation on July 4, 1776 were really not the first democracy on the American continent.

More than 2,000 years before that, the ideas of human equality, cooperation, and freedom had already taken root.

We are now at home.

From now on we shall take only short trips through Time, and will meet some very remarkable persons.

The best is yet to come.

I promise wondrous events before we reach the end.

But remember this: All endings are really only beginnings.

# THIRTEEN

# THE PROMISED LAND
## Just Before Dawn

This must be said first: Most of the early explorers to this new world came because of greed. They had heard tales of fabulous treasures of gold and silver and precious jewels.

I'd better say this right now, too; along with the Spanish conquerors came the priests, who were eager to convert what they called "savages" to the Christian faith. It grieves me to tell you that some of these priests tortured and murdered the natives who resisted. They burned libraries and destroyed old historical records. Sad, isn't it?

But in time that too passed away and better men and women began to flock to these new lands. They came from France, Holland, and England, and formed colonies which drew more and more of their countrymen.

The English effort was led by our old friend Sir Francis Bacon, who saw that here in North America was the land of his dreams, the perfect setting for his ideal democracy . . . The Promised Land.

Just think; we are part of Bacon's dream, and we live here and now in that same Promised Land.

After the Conquistadors had done their damage, the settlers of the new colonies came to these shores in search of freedom, escaping from persecution in the Old World.

But many of them, after becoming free in this New World, began to force their ideas of Freedom on the others. In so doing, they were just as bad as what they had left behind. You see, they had not really changed just because they were here. They were the same persons, and were sure their own ideas were right.

One of the "secret fires" was lit by Francis Bacon. The flame from that group flared quickly and burned brightly, attracting leaders and their followers from Germany, France, and Holland as well as from England.

Pennsylvania, a state founded and named by William Penn, an English Quaker, was where many of the Torch-Bearers gathered.

One leader, a German named Kelpius, arrived in Philadelphia (which means "brotherly love") and lived for years in a cave. Kelpius and his followers brought with them books written by a German named Jacob Boehme (pronounced "bay-me"). Kelpius' group were Pietists, which was a religious movement started back in Germany. Their main book was called *An ABC Book for Young Students Studying in the College of the Holy Ghost*. They brought two other curious names to this new world—"The Order of the Mustard Seed" and "Order of the Woman in the Wilderness."

It was a time of new movements and great experiments in human dignity and freedom.

By the 18th century, most of the colonies were English, and the towns springing up were much like villages back in England.

The Torch-Bearers held their secret meetings in rooms over inns and other public buildings.

The Old and New Worlds of the Eastern and Western Hemispheres were on their way to becoming One World, and Bacon and his followers were getting America ready to lead the search for freedom in this One World. Isn't it fascinating to watch the Dawn of the New Day?

Future leaders were being born here in America itself. One was a man we all know—Benjamin Franklin. He was born in Boston in 1706. Boston was then a small town of a few thousand people.

Franklin, who has been called "The First American Gentleman," was most unusual. He was not a military leader, and never became President, but he was one of the most important men in the fight for independence.

He was an inventor, a printer, a scientist, and a philosopher. Many of his ideas were printed in his famous *Poor Richard's Almanack,* which was read by philosophers as well as by farmers.

He was Minister to France, and his signature is in the records of a French secret society called "Lodge of Perfection."

Where else can his signature be seen? Why, on the Declaration of Independence, of course.

So Franklin was very important in the founding of this country, and we'll learn more about him later on.

New Atlantis was born.

After 150 years, Bacon's dreams were beginning to come true.

On July 4, 1776, the freedom of man was announced to the world.

This freedom is infinite as long as we conform to Law.

Someone has defined freedom as "voluntary servitude to universal law," and it extends to the farthest reaches of

Time and Space.

I'm reminded of the time Mrs. Albert Einstein was being shown through a modern observatory. When she was escorted to the dome, with its large telescope and complicated mechanisms, she asked, "What is the purpose of this enormous machine?"

The astronomer replied, "Why, to explore the boundaries of the universe."

Her answer, with a smile, was, "My husband did that on the back of an envelope."

Looking ahead I see strange writings, somewhat like the ones Nostradamus wrote—hard to understand, but of great interest.

The meanings have been explained for us, so we should have fun in studying them.

They are prophecies written at the time the Father of our country, George Washington, was born.

And they are also *about* George Washington and leaders who came along later.

Ready? Let's go!

# FOURTEEN

# THE 1732 PROPHECY
## We Work on a Great Puzzle

George Washington was born in Virginia in 1732.

In that same year, in Scotland, a man named Sir William Hope wrote down a vision he had, which we'll read and discuss and try to understand.

Sir William wrote his verses on the blank pages of a book he published eight years before. The name of the book is *Vindication of the True Art of Self Defense*.

The book is in the Library of Congress.

The book itself is not important to us, but the verses he wrote certainly are.

Remember, the year was 1732.

George Washington had just been born.

It was 44 years before the Revolutionary War.

And there were thirteen American colonies which had not yet begun to think of independence.

Some of the signers of the Declaration of Independence had not yet been born.

Here is Sir William's first verse:

I'll write these just the way they are written in his book.

Listen!

Preface

'Tis Chaldee says his fate is great
Whose stars do bear him fortunate.
Of thy near fate, Amerika,
I read in stars a prophecy:
Fourteen divided, twelve the same,
Sixteen in halfs—each holds a name;
Four, eight, seven, six—added ten—
The life-line's mark of Four gt. men.

Let's see what we can make of that. . . .

Sir William is giving us the first clue to four great (gt.) men in America.

Their names were to be divided into fourteen letters, twelve letters, and sixteen letters.

And their lives would add up to 250. You see, by "four, eight, seven, six—added ten" we were to add the four numbers . . . that's 25, and then *multiply* by ten to give us 250. And we can find the four Americans whose names and lives fit those numbers. Checking, we find . . . Washington lived for 68 years, Lincoln for 56, Benjamin Harrison for 68, and McKinley for 58.

68, 56, 68, 58 . . . those add up to 250.

Then he wrote:

A Prophecy

This day is cradled, far beyond the sea,
One starred by fate to rule both bond and free.

Remember, this was written the year of Washington's birth, so that part is easy.

By "bond and free" he meant that slavery would still be present in Washington's time. "Bond" means chained or shackled.

Next we read:

> Add double four, thus fix the destined day
> When servile knees unbend 'neath freedom's sway.

By adding "double four," 44, to 1732, we get 1776, the year of the Declaration of Independence!

And then:

> Place six 'fore ten, then read the patriot's name
> Whose deeds shall link him to a deathless fame.

There are six letters in "George" and ten letters in "Washington."

Let's read on:

> Whose growing love and ceaseless trust wrong none
> And catch truth's colors from its glowing sun!
> Death's door shall clang while yet his century waits,
> His planets point the way to others' pending fates.

Those four lines are a tribute to Washington, and the third line, "Death's door shall clang while yet his century waits," is a prophecy, for Washington died on December 14, 1799, shortly before the end of the eighteenth century.

Following are two more very interesting lines on Washington:

> Till all the names on freedom's scroll shall fade,
> Two tombs be built, his lofty cenotaph be made.

Really, those two lines are easy. "Freedom's scroll" is, of course, the Declaration of Independence, and the names written on it have begun to fade. And Washington's body has rested in two tombs.

The "lofty cenotaph"—what would that be? Well, a

cenotaph is a monument erected to someone buried in some other location and . . . you've guessed it, of course; it's the Washington Monument.

And is it "lofty"? It certainly is! It's 555 feet high, the tallest monument ever built in the memory of a man.

And then comes:

> Full six times ten the years must onward glide,
> Nature their potent help—a constant, prudent guide.

"Six times ten," 60, added to the year Washington died, gives us 1859. That's the year of an event that led to the great Civil War—the hanging of John Brown, who was caught raiding Harper's Ferry, trying to free the slaves.

There's much more. Let's read on:

> Then fateful seven 'fore seven shall sign heroic son
> Whom Mars and Jupiter strike down before his work is done.
> When cruel fate shall pierce, though artless of its sword;
> Who leaves life's gloomy stage without one final word.
> A softly beaming star, half veiled by Mars' red cloud
> Virtue, his noblest cloak, shall form a fitting shroud.

Those six lines are packed with meaning, but with a little digging they become clear.

There are seven letters in "Abraham" and seven letters in "Lincoln," who was certainly a "heroic son," elected President in 1860 and re-elected in 1864.

And he was "struck down before his work was done." He was shot and killed on April 14, 1865.

Look at the line "Who leaves life's gloomy stage without one final word." Lincoln was shot in a theater while watching a stage play, and died several hours later without having said a word.

And a shroud is a cloak which covers the dead; wouldn't "Virtue," Lincoln's "noblest cloak," be a proper shroud?

The next two lines read:

Then eight 'fore eight a later generation rules,
With light undimmed and shed in progress' school.

There are eight letters in "Benjamin" and eight letters in "Harrison."

And he did rule as President in a "later generation," 1889 to 1893. His administration was not dimmed by war or scandal.

The great Columbian Exposition was held in Chicago in 1893. It was an exhibit of progress made in invention, transportation, industry, art, science, and agriculture during the country's first 100 years. That would be the "progress' school" referred to.

Let's read the next four lines of Hope's poem:

Then six again, with added six shall rise,
Resplendent ruler—good, and great—and wise.
Four sixes hold a glittering star that on his way shall shine;
And twice four sixes mark his years from birth to manhood's prime.

President McKinley's family name, when divided into "Will-Mc" and "Kinley," means "Will, son of Kinley." That gives us the "six with added six" in the first line.

And "four sixes"? McKinley was the twenty-fourth

man to become President.

And "twice four sixes"? McKinley was 48 at his "prime" when he was elected Governor of Ohio.

McKinley's death—he was shot and killed in 1901—was not included in the verse, because the prophecies ended before the next century had begun, as we see in the last four lines of the poem:

> These truths prophetic shall completion see
> Ere time's deep grave receives the Nineteenth Century!
> All planets, stars, twelve signs and horoscope
> Attest these certain truths foretold by William Hope.

That book has been in the Library of Congress for over 100 years now.

How did Sir William make those prophecies?

I certainly don't know.*

Well, let's look ahead . . . what do we see fluttering so proudly in the breeze? Why, it's our country's flag! And there's a mystery surrounding that, too!

---

*The complete poem is included at the end of this book.

# FIFTEEN

# THE MYSTERIOUS PROFESSOR AND THE STARS AND STRIPES
## How Our Flag Was Born

This is a story of three centuries:

ONE—About 300 years ago, Sir Francis Bacon made a rule that every book written in the name of the Order of the Quest should be marked in a special way so that other members would recognize it.

TWO—Over 200 years ago, in 1775, four famous men met with a mysterious stranger in a house in Massachusetts to design a flag for America.

THREE—Almost 100 years ago, a book was written about that flag and that meeting. The book is called *Our Flag, or the Evolution of the Stars and Stripes.* The last sentence in the book is a quote from Bacon, and the last word in the book is . . . Bacon.

It's very likely that the ending was one of Bacon's "marks" so that other of the Torch-Bearers would recognize it. We know very little about the author of the book, Robert Allen Campbell. Only a few copies were printed, and evidently the information in the chapter about the colonial flag was told to him.

Here is the story about "The Colonial Flag":

Benjamin Franklin, Benjamin Harrison, and Thomas

Lynch were appointed by Congress to design a flag for the colonies. By the way, all three men, one year later, were to sign their names to our Declaration of Independence.

They traveled to Cambridge, Massachusetts to consult with General George Washington, who was in an army camp there.

During their stay in Cambridge, the three men were guests in a home there. The owners already had one guest, an elderly man called simply "The Professor." He and Dr. Franklin shared one room, and the other two men shared a spare guest room.

On the night of the first day, December 13, 1775, the host and hostess gave a dinner for the new arrivals. General Washington and The Professor were present also.

The three committeemen held their first meeting after the dinner, with Washington and the host present. Dr. Franklin invited The Professor to join in also.

The Professor's first suggestion was to include their hostess too, so that made seven members; a "better number," said The Professor, "than the number six." They appointed her as secretary of the committee.

They met again next evening, December 14, in The Professor's room.

General Washington opened the meeting by calling upon Dr. Franklin, who in turn asked The Professor to speak.

The Professor compared the coming days of our country to the dark depressing days of the coming winter. But he knew that both the country and the sun would gain in strength with the arrival of spring and reach a new height, a "glorious culmination" by the summertime.

Remember; the Declaration of Independence was to be signed the coming July 4, 1776!

Then he went on to say that the new country would continue to grow until it was as strong as any on this earth, and he knew that the flag designed for such a young, growing country would have to be designed in a way which would exhibit a source of strength and stability plus one other thing . . . part of it must be left open for the changes which he saw coming ahead.

So here was the flag they designed:

A flag of thirteen stripes, red and white, one for each of the colonies. That part would remain for the strong idealistic beginning.

The section where the changes would take place was the blue area in the upper left hand corner that now contains the 50 stars. At that time it held the flag of Great Britain, the "Union Jack," which consists of the two crosses of England and Scotland (the crosses of Saint George and Saint Andrew) superimposed.

Do you suppose there will be any more stars added in that blue section with the passage of time?

That flag was first raised by General Washington himself in Cambridge, Massachusetts on the first days of the new year, and it was cheered by both the British and the colonists.

Six months later the Declaration of Independence was announced to the world.

And one year after that, on June 14, 1777, the circle of thirteen stars replaced the Union Jack. That day, June 14, is now annually observed as "Flag Day."

Just think of all the people who worked and fought to get this nation started. Some are well known, but others are mysterious, shadowy figures who seem to appear at the right places and the right times purely by chance.

The Professor was one of them.

And we'll be seeing more of them.

Just wait.

SIXTEEN
# THE TORCH-BEARER WHO ALMOST LOST HIS HEAD
## The Story of a Fighter

Thirty-nine years before the Declaration of Independence, a boy was born in England to a family of Quakers, a religious sect called "Society of Friends." Thomas Paine—that was the boy's name—never finished grammar school, yet had a lot to do with America's fight for independence from England.

In 1774, when he was 37, he met Benjamin Franklin in England, and decided to come to America. That was just two years before the Declaration of Independence.

Then, early in 1776, he wrote a short essay called *Common Sense,* which stirred up the colonists in their struggle. And we are sure he must have worked with Thomas Jefferson on the document itself. The words "Laws of Nature" and "Nature's God" on the final draft are probably his.

"These are times that try men's souls" was an expression of his that became a battle cry.

Paine held government jobs in the new nation for the next few years. Then, in 1789, he sailed back to England, where he soon got into trouble. In 1791 he wrote a famous essay called *Rights of Man,* which caused such an uproar that he was to be tried for treason. But he had a very good friend, a poet named William Blake, who helped him escape to France before the trial began.

Once there, he soon found himself in real trouble again. He joined the French Revolution, but he was too broad-minded for the French Terrorists, who threw him into prison. You see, he had opposed the execution of King Louis XVI. So what did the enraged terrorists plan for our friend Paine? Death itself! And by what means? By a terrible invention called the guillotine. And what was this guillotine? Why, it was a sharp, heavy blade made to fall from a great height and strike the victim at the back of the neck.

That's how Tom almost lost his head!

But he was lucky. The leader of the French Revolution, a man named Robespierre, lost his power and the new leaders released him.

And what did Tom do then? He rejoined the Revolution!

Oh, he was a fighter, all right!

While in prison in France, Paine had finished writing his book *Age of Reason,* which described his Quaker views on separation of Church and State. He believed that all religions are good when not mixed in with government and politics.

He returned to America in 1802, but even then got into a bit of trouble here through his attacks on George Washington.

You see, he believed that Washington and the Americans had deserted him while he was in prison in France.

He died in 1809. Ten years later his body was sent back to England for re-burial there.

Thomas Paine fought corruption wherever he found it, in government, in politics, in religion. He fought with skill and honesty. No wonder he was in trouble so often. His influence was great because he expressed strong views in simple, direct language easily understood.

He was far ahead of his time.

We need people "ahead of their time," don't we? Their torches burn clear and bright, making it easier for us to see better.

He believed we are all free and created equal, with a right to be heard and a right to equal enjoyment of the bounties of Nature.

He was an idealist and a perfectionist.

He refused to accept man's weaknesses. That's probably why he attacked President Washington. Even great leaders are only human, and cannot be expected to be perfect.

He refused to back down one inch.

He was a Utopian.


Thomas Paine had many narrow escapes in his 72 years, but there was always someone (or some thing) which rescued him "just in the nick of time."

Perhaps he was being guided from above.

This we do know: When the dream of world democracy does come true, the name of Thomas Paine will be there for all to see, written in letters of fire.


Perhaps Tom Paine was guided by one of those mysterious unknowns.

Coming up is a quick encounter with another one.

We still don't know who he was.

# SEVENTEEN

# THE SPEAKER IN THE BALCONY
## And Our "Golden Fleece"

Early one morning in the year 1776, a number of men were observed streaming into the old State House in Philadelphia.

Why were they gathering on that particular day?

To declare that the American Colonies were, and ought to be, free and independent.

The day was July 4.

It was an important day for us now as well as for them then.

It was also dangerous, and called for great courage on the part of the delegates.

You see, if the Revolution failed, all these men who signed their names to that document would be tried for treason, subject to the death penalty.

Also, these were men of vastly differing backgrounds and opinions from all sections of the young nation.

They had to reach common agreement, not at all easy to do.

After all were assembled, and with a number of spectators seated in the balcony to observe the proceedings, the doors were locked and a guard posted outside.

Then the speeches, debates, and arguments began.

Thomas Jefferson, John Adams, and Benjamin Franklin spoke.

All that time, with all the speech-making going on, the document lay on the table, ready for signing. But many of the delegates had not yet decided to sign.

The Library of Congress has letters written by Thomas Jefferson about the day's events.

Late in the day, many of the delegates were still fearful, with that possible death penalty lingering in their minds.

The time was at hand for a decision to be made, one way or another.

Right at that moment, according to a rare old book of political speeches, a man in the balcony sprang to his feet and made a speech that shocked the delegates into action.

His first word was "Gibbet!" That's pronounced "jib-bit," and is a word for gallows, a framework of wood from which convicted criminals were hanged.

You see, the speakers had been using that word, and the man in the balcony had heard enough and knew the time had come for action.

He want on to say (and I here use my own words, not the speech as printed in the book):*

". . . they may stretch our necks on every tree and make every home a grave, but the words on that document can never die!

---

*See *The Secret Destiny of America,* by Manly P. Hall.

"Those are words of God! What care we of the British king!

"Long after our bones are dust, those words will still live. To the laborer they speak hope; to the slave, freedom; but to the coward king they speak a warning!

"Sign that document! Sign, even if we are hung tomorrow! Sign or be cursed forever! Sign for yourselves, for us, for all ages to come! That document is the Book of Wisdom, the Bible of the Rights of Man!

"Don't be afraid! Don't whisper in fear! Look to God and your own hearts! Look what we few have done already! We are few but we are mighty! Look at Bunker Hill! God has meant America to be free!

"The old world is drenched with blood and staggering in the dark. But God says, 'Let there be Light.'

"My friends, we are making a new world, a new world of Freedom and Light for the enslaved millions struggling in the darkness of the old world.

"That document is the Voice of God, my friends, and I beg you with all my heart, even if it were with my last breath, to remember . . . God intends America to be free!

"Yes, with my last faint whisper, I beg you to sign for the sake of the millions who look to you to say to them . . . 'You are free'!"

The man fell back exhausted as the delegates rushed to sign.

With a bold flourish, John Hancock signed first, handed it to another who signed it and handed it on to another, then another, then another. . . .

It was done.

The delegates then turned to thank the speaker in the balcony.

He wasn't there.

We don't know who he was. The people around him either didn't know or never said.

How did he happen to be at just the right place and time? And how did he disappear so suddenly?

Only his speech remains in a rare little book.

He mentioned "rights of man." Thomas Paine's book of that name came thirteen years later.

He looks very much like another of our Light-Bearers.

Many great events in history have come about through efforts of persons unknown.

A history of Light-Bearers would contain many famous people like Sir Francis Bacon, but it would also have many more unknown men and women who helped tremendously.

The Order of the Quest asks its members to adopt the customs of the countries to which they travel and to work quietly without attracting attention.

One of these mysterious strangers was "The Professor" who helped design our flag.

Another was "the speaker in the balcony."

You and I can do our part to help in the Great Plan, even if in very small ways.

After all, devoted men and women as far back as Plato, and even farther, laid the plans for New Atlantis.

We should be proud and willing to carry a little of the Light.

With deep gratitude for the brave men who signed their names on our "Golden Fleece," and with special thanks to "the speaker in the balcony," we now look ahead to where we shall see our Founding Fathers still working diligently in a most fascinating chapter of our early history.

# EIGHTEEN

# THE GREAT SEAL
## How the Phoenix Bird Became an Eagle

Right after the Declaration of Independence was signed, the Continental Congress appointed Benjamin Franklin, John Adams, and Thomas Jefferson to design a seal for use on State documents.

The word "seal" comes from a Latin word meaning "sign" or "symbol."

In August, just one month later, the three men were ready with their design and submitted it to Congress.

It was not approved, but three parts of it were saved. Those three parts were: (1) the motto "one out of many," (2) an eye in a triangle, and (3) the date, 1776.

In 1780 another design was submitted. It also was not approved, but again, three parts of it were retained. They were: (1) the thirteen stripes on a shield, (2) the olive branch, and (3) the circle of thirteen stars.

A third committee sent one more design to Congress. In that design, two more symbols—the eagle and the pyramid—appeared for the first time.

When Benjamin Franklin looked it over, he approved, saying that "the wild turkey" was a good choice!

Yes, he thought the bird on the drawing was a turkey. And he was disappointed when told that the bird was an eagle. He pointed out that the eagle is a bird of prey. "Besides," he said, "it doesn't look like an eagle."

What really was the bird on that drawing?

It was a Phoenix.

The Phoenix resembles an eagle in size, but has a longer neck, different shaped beak, different feather coloring, and a tuft of feathers on the back of the head. That great seal of 1782 shows a crested Phoenix, with neck and beak smaller than they are now.

The story of the Phoenix is interesting. You'll find it in stories from many countries and times. It's mentioned in what may have been Shakespeare's last play, *The Tempest*.

It is an ancient sign of the Order of the Quest.

Legend has it that only one Phoenix lives at a time. It lives for 500 years, and when it dies, its body opens and a new Phoenix is born.

It is the symbol of everlasting life.

When a person becomes wise he is said to be "born again." In olden times, those accepted into the temple were said to be "twice-born" or "born again."

The Phoenix is a sign of power and has been used by many nations. The Phoenix of China has the same meaning as the Phoenix of Egypt, and the Greek Phoenix is the same as the "Thunder Bird" of the American Indians.

Get a dollar bill and look closely and carefully at it. You'll find some very interesting words and pictures on it. We use these dollars all the time, but rarely stop to take a good look at them.

On the front we see a picture of George Washington,

and on the back are shown both sides of the great seal of the United States.

In the middle, over the large ONE, we see IN GOD WE TRUST.

On the left side is the back of the great seal, showing the Great Pyramid of Gizah. At the base is the date 1776 in Roman numerals—MDCCLXXVI.

There are 13 layers of stones in the pyramid.

On the flat top of the pyramid is the "All-Seeing Eye in a Radiant Triangle."

Incidentally, a Harvard professor, Charles Norton, didn't like the pyramid symbol. He said it looked like a Masonic emblem. That bit of information is to be found in a book published in 1909, *The History of the Seal of the United States,* by Gaillard Hunt.

The ancient Egyptians believed the Pyramid of Gizah to be the tomb of Hermes (Thot), god of wisdom.

The Great Pyramid was left unfinished, with a flat top.

The pyramid is man himself. And isn't man imperfect and unfinished?

The first three letters of "pyramid" come from a Greek word meaning "fire." So here we are with "fire" again! The pyramid is a symbol of the Magic Fire. And we humans are keepers of that Flame.

The All-Seeing Eye is a symbol of the Order of the Quest.

The triangle in the shape of the Greek letter "D" (delta) is the first letter of the four-letter name of God. Our word "deity" comes from a Latin word "Deus," meaning "God."

The Hebrews use the word tetragrammaton. "Tetra"

means "four" and "grammaton" means "letter."

It's the four-letter name for God . . . JHVH . . . which is "Jehovah" without the vowels "e," "o," and "a."

I'm told those four letters, JHVH, can be arranged in 72 ways.

I haven't tried it, I just take their word for it. Here's another interesting fact: There are 72 stones in that pyramid on the dollar bill!

The pyramid is also the House of the Universe, with God above, observing all Creation.

Over the All-Seeing Eye on the dollar bill are the words ANNUIT COEPTIS. That means "God Approves."

Under the pyramid are the words NOVUS ORDO SE-CLORUM. Those words mean "A New Order for the Ages."

By the way, there is a legend that in old Atlantis was a great university in the shape of a pyramid, with an observatory on top.

Now look at the right side of the dollar bill. That is the front of the great seal showing the eagle (once a Phoenix).

In his beak is a banner with E PLURIBUS UNUM on it— Latin for "one out of many." His right talon holds an olive branch, the symbol of peace, and his left a sheaf of 13 arrows.

Over the eagle's head we see a crest of 13 stars.

The body of the eagle is covered by a shield of 13 stripes.

Who said that 13 is unlucky?

That's quite a story, isn't it?

But that's not all.

That great seal design was approved way back in 1782, more than 200 years ago, but the back side with the pyramid was not used for many years.

Why? Because it was thought to be a symbol of some secret society.

And they were right.

It was a symbol used by our Light-Bearers, members of the Order of the Quest.

It was not until 1935 that most Americans ever saw that pyramid. That's when it first appeared on the dollar bill.

It was time that symbol appeared, as the world was heading right into the terrible years of World War II, threatening the survival of democracy. A tyrant, Adolf Hitler, was coming to power in Germany, and there was darkness everywhere.


The Phoenix, the Pyramid, and the All-Seeing Eye— those three symbols came to this land with the Light-Bearers 150 years before the Revolution.

They were the early patriots who inspired the design on our great seal.

And those early patriots got their inspiration from the Ancient Wisdom.

This land of ours is meant to be a nation of Light-Bearers, ruled over by God and dedicated to seeing that his will be done.

When we know this and dedicate our own lives, this nation will shine like a living torch, inspiring all other nations.

I'll show you the Living Symbol of that living torch when we reach the end of our Journey.

We must be faithful to the trust handed down to us. Not to do so would be to throw away a priceless gift.

We shall not fail.

We now approach our last two adventures.

We shall learn of our country's darkest hour, and we shall see how, once again, we were rescued by another shadowy figure "just in the nick of time."

NINETEEN
# GENERAL McCLELLAN'S DREAM
## A Rescue by the Father of Our Country

Merlin, the wizard in the legendary days of King Arthur's court in England, predicted that a maid would arise in France to do great deeds for that country.

Several hundred years later that prophecy came true in the person of Joan of Arc, who led French forces in decisive battles against the English in the early fifteenth century.

She proclaimed herself a Messenger of God, and was directed by voices she had heard as early as her thirteenth year. At the age of sixteen she was told to go to the French leaders and direct the rescue of the city of Orleans from the English siege.

That is one of many stories of visions and dreams coming to persons in the past which have changed the course of history.

Now here is one you might not know about, but it too had a profound effect upon our nation's history and came at a very crucial time. The story was printed in a newspaper, the *Evening Courier,* in Portland, Maine, on March 8, 1862.

That, of course, was right in the midst of our Civil War.

General McClellan had just arrived in Washington to

take command of the U.S. Army.

It was after midnight of his third day there, and he had fallen asleep while studying maps spread out on the table before him.

Then the door—which had been locked—opened and a voice spoke to him.

This was at a time when the country was deeply divided. President Lincoln was in the White House, trying desperately to save the Union.

Following is the story, in my own words, of what took place in McClellan's office that night.

Here is what the voice said to him:

"General, do you sleep at your post? Wake up! or your enemies will be in Washington!"

McClellan felt as though he was suspended in space, with the voice coming from every direction. He started to rise, but whether awake or still sleeping, he did not know.

The table with its maps was still before him, but the rest of the room had disappeared.

In its place was a living map of the whole country between the Mississippi River and the Atlantic Ocean.

He was unable to see the face of the man speaking to him.

The General looked more closely at the great map. There he could see the enemy troops, spread out across the land, advancing toward Washington!

He was excited to see his enemies so clearly, but then he noticed that those troops were heading directly toward the points he meant to occupy in the next few days. He became agitated, realizing that spies had been taking his plans directly to his enemies.

The voice then spoke again:

"General McClellan, you have very little time. By sunrise, without the help of God, your enemy's flag will wave over our nation's capital . . . and your grave!"

McClellan swiftly marked down the enemy's positions on the paper map on the table. When he finished, he looked up . . . into the face of George Washington!

Then our First President went on to say, in a slow, solemn voice,

"General McClellan, I saw this nation begin. Less than one hundred years have passed.

"This is our nation's darkest hour. She must win through and take her rightful place among the great nations of the world.

"But with victory the mission is not ended. Before another hundred years, she will be in a great world war. If victorious then, she will increase in power and prosperity and lead the world to democracy.

"But she must always remember to place her trust in God. Then she will never fail."

Washington raised his hand in farewell, there was a clap of thunder in space, and McClellan woke with a start.

The living map had disappeared and the room was back as it had been.

His map was still on the table.

But it was now covered with new markings.

He walked around the room in a daze.

Was he awake now, or still dreaming? Had he really seen President Washington?

He went back and looked at the map again.

Yes, the new markings he had made were there.

He immediately saddled his horse and rode from camp to camp, giving orders for the next day's battles.

It was just in time. The city of Washington had been saved, but the enemy had come so close that Abraham Lincoln, sitting at his desk in the White House, could hear the rumble of the guns of the Confederate Army.

Later, after all the units had been alerted, General McClellan gave a prayer of thanks as he pictured President Washington lying peacefully in his tomb until a next dark hour when he might again be needed as a Messenger of God.

The future was unknown to McClellan, but he knew the map he had marked during his vision would always be a reminder of the debt this nation owes to God and the spirit of Washington.

He then knew that this nation had to have a secret destiny.

Exploring that destiny is what our own little Journey through Time and Space has been about.

General McClellan's dream took place more than 100 years ago.

Since then we have been in, not just one, but two World Wars, in which tyrannies have tried to destroy democracy.

We have come through to lead the free world.

We must continue to keep the dreams of the Light-Bearers.

Whenever changes are badly needed in times of crisis, messengers appear in dreams and visions. Are they spirits of the dead returning?

Or, is man able to reach out with his own spirit and find the Truth?

This we do know: Men and women have had visions and heard guiding voices in times of danger.

May it always be so.

Now wasn't that a story to stir your imagination and lift your spirits?

And won't it always be a source of inspiration to us?


It is with a touch of sadness that I tell you our Journey together is almost over.

I hope you have enjoyed it as much as I have.

But, looking ahead, I see one more Light, a scene of shining hope, a vision of our future dreams.

Once more, let's go.

# TWENTY

# THE NEW COLOSSUS
## End of Our Journey

In ancient times any giant statue was called a "colossus."

The most famous one was the bronze statue of the sun-god Helios at the entrance to the harbor on the island of Rhodes in the Aegean Sea.

That statue, over 100 feet high, held a burning torch in its hand, serving as a beacon for ships approaching the City of Rhodes. It was toppled by an earthquake in 224 B.C.

Now before I show you The New Colossus let's wrap things up a bit about our Journey together.

Philosophy tells us that real progress takes place inside each one of us.

That's where real evolution occurs, not in the complicated social structures man has created again and again.

Why did the League of Nations fail?

It failed because the nations didn't dream true.

Today we have the United Nations, struggling along, partly succeeding, sometimes failing.

We can still make it succeed. Only time will tell.

True growth comes from education, not laws.

And education must teach ideals.

It must teach each young person how to make a *life,* rather than just how to make a "living."

If our aims are right, we are educated.

If our aims are wrong, we are *un*educated, no matter how many years we went to school.

There are three ways to learn: (1) by Studying, (2) by Seeing, and (3) by Doing.

Only the wise can really lead. The rest of us must help.

When a ruler is wise, the people say, "We did it ourselves."

The best state has few basic laws.

Where there are too many laws, there are too many law *breakers.*

Besides, New Atlantis can't become a reality just by passing laws.

What is freedom? Is it doing whatever we please?

No. Freedom is the right to do the things we should do, plus "pleasing" to do those same things.

Today we live in a time of half truths, which is why we fall so often.

Religion, philosophy, and science—these are the three parts of learning.

Once they were united.

They can be united again.

Religion is the spiritual part.

Philosophy is the mental part.

Science is the physical part.

We are spirit, mind, and body, aren't we?

So we are One. Learning should be One also.

When we're out of balance we fall, don't we?

Plato taught that all these parts must be used in the search for Truth.

Why are those ancient Light-Bearers still so highly respected?

Because each one was a "priest-philosopher-scientist."

When those three parts are united in one person, that person is wise.


It's up to us to build the perfect society, the "college of the six day's work" (remember?). That college would still teach the same things as today, but with this difference: It would teach that—

Science is as sacred as Religion, and

Philosophy is as practical as trades and crafts.

Do you understand?

Then, our "secret university" would be secret no longer.

Nation after nation has risen and fallen. Do you remember, back when we started on our Journey together, we learned that the life of a nation seems to last about 250 years?

Well, our own nation is now just over 200 years old, so you can see there's a challenge ahead of you.

The time of decision has come.

Mother Nature is waiting.

It's up to you.

God is revealed through Mother Nature.

That is where you must search.

It's up to you.

The Light-Bearers will keep on working in secret until their dreams come true.

The University of the Six Days' Work is to be built right here to guide all nations.

Isn't that a beautiful dream?

The dream can come true.

It's up to you.

Well, my Companion, our Journey together is over.

But in the distance is a giant Torch-Bearer, holding high the Lamp of Hope, Freedom, and Liberty.

Yes, it's the Statue of Liberty in New York Harbor.

At the base of the statue is the poem I promised you when we began. Here it is:

### THE NEW COLOSSUS
Not like the brazen giant of Greek fame,
With conquering limbs astride from land to land,
Here at our sea-washed, sunset-gates shall stand
A mighty woman with a torch, whose flame
Is the imprisoned lightning, and her name
Mother of Exiles. From her beacon-hand
Glows world-wide welcome, her mild eyes command
The air-bridged harbor that twin-cities frame.

"Keep, ancient lands, your storied pomp!" cries she,
With silent lips. "Give me your tired, your poor,
Your huddled masses yearning to breathe free,
The wretched refuse of your teeming shore,—
Send these, the homeless, tempest-tost to me,
I lift my lamp beside the golden door!"

Beautiful, isn't it? That was written by a woman named Emma Lazarus, on November 2, 1883, over one hundred years ago.

The time has come for us to part, but the secret of the Magic Fire still holds—remember?

And haven't we been together with every word you read?

Now, from one twentieth-century Truth-Seeker to another,

Goodbye and a Happy Journey!

Keep your Light shining bright!

It's up to you.

# ADDENDUM

Here is the complete poem as written in Sir William Hope's book (see page 63).

Preface.

'Tis Chaldee says his fate is great
Whose stars do bear him fortunate.
Of thy near fate, Amerika,
I read in stars a prophecy:
Fourteen divided, twelve the same,
Sixteen in halfs—each holds a name;
Four, eight, seven, six—added ten—
The life-line's mark of Four gt. men.

A Prophecy

This day is cradled, far beyond the sea,
One starred by fate to rule both bond and free;
Add double four, thus fix the destined day
When servile knees unbend 'neath freedom's sway.
Place six 'fore ten, then read the patriot's name,
Whose deeds shall link him to a deathless fame,
Whose glowing love and ceaseless trust wrong none,
And catch truth's colors from its glowing sun!
Death's door shall clang while yet his century waits,
His planets point the way to others' pending fates.
Till all the names on freedom's scroll shall fade,
Two tombs be built, his lofty cenotaph be made.
Full six times ten the years must onward glide,
Nature their potent help,—a constant, prudent guide.
Then fateful seven 'fore seven shall sign heroic son
Whom Mars and Jupiter strike down before his work is done.
When cruel fate shall pierce, though artless of its sword;
Who leaves life's gloomy stage without one final word.
A softly beaming star, half veiled by Mars' red cloud
Virtue, his noblest cloak, shall form a fitting shroud.
Then eight 'fore eight a later generation rules,

With light undimmed and shed in progress' school.
Then six again, with added six shall rise,
Resplendent ruler—good, and great—and wise.
Four sixes hold a glittering star that on his way shall shine;
And twice four sixes mark his years from birth to manhood's prime.

These truths prophetic shall completion see
Ere time's deep grave receives the nineteenth century!
All planets, stars, twelve signs and horoscope
Attest these certain truths foretold by William Hope.
                            Writ at Cornhill, London, 1732.

A descendant of Sir William's added, in some later year, the following four lines in a blank space at the bottom of the page:

The learned hand that writ these lines no more shall pen for me,
Yet voice shall speak and pulses beat for long posterity.
This soul refined through love of kind bewailed life's labors spent,
Then found this truth, his search from youth, greatness is God's
   accident. . .
                                        James Hope